OCCO

D1532053

The CASABLANCA COOKBOOK

WINING AND DINING AT RICK'S

SARAH KEY

JENNIFER NEWMAN BRAZIL

VICKI WELLS

ABBEVILLE PRESS PUBLISHERS

New York · London · Paris

ILLUSTRATIONS, MAP, AND PAGE BORDERS:
Devyne Design
DESIGNER: Patricia Fabricant
PRODUCTION MANAGER: Dana Cole
COPYEDITOR: Amy Handy

A special thanks to Diane Simone Vezza and Zachary Meisel
for assistance in recipe testing and development.

Also available in the Hollywood Hotplates series:
A Christmas Carol Cookbook
Gone With The Wind Cook Book™
The "I Love Lucy"™ *Cookbook*
The Wizard of Oz™ *Cookbook*

First edition
10 9 8 7 6 5 4 3

Library of Congress Cataloging-in-Publication Data
Key, Sarah.
    The Casablanca cookbook : wining and dining at Rick's / Sarah
Key, Jennifer Newman Brazil, Vicky Wells.
        p.   cm.
    ISBN 1-55859-474-4
    1. Cookery, Moroccan. 2. Casablanca (Motion picture) I. Brazil,
Jennifer Newman. II. Wells, Vicki. III. Title.
TX725.M8K49 1992
641.5964—dc20   92-26458

METRIC CONVERSIONS: 1 teaspoon = 5 ml; 1 tablespoon = 14.8 ml.

CONTENTS

FAMOUS COCKTAILS, FRUIT DRINKS, AND TEMPTING TIDBITS

*"Of all the gin joints in all
the towns in all the world,
she walks into mine!"*

"Here's Looking at You, Kid" Champagne Cocktail

*SAM: This sort of takes the sting out of being
occupied, doesn't it, Mr. Richard?*

*2 teaspoons granulated sugar
2 ounces (60 ml) blood-orange juice
(regular orange juice can be substituted)
2 teaspoons lime juice, freshly squeezed
4 ounces (120 ml) champagne or sparkling wine
lime wedge*

Place sugar in a chilled champagne flute. Add juices and
stir to dissolve sugar. Top glass with champagne. Garnish
with lime wedge.

MAKES 1 DRINK.

Raspberry Champagne Kiss

*1 tablespoon Chambord (or other
black-raspberry-flavored brandy)
4 ounces (120 ml) dry champagne
2 fresh raspberries*

Pour Chambord into a chilled champagne flute. Add chilled
champagne and garnish with raspberries. Serve immediately.

MAKES 1 DRINK.

White Wine Spritzer

4 ounces (120 ml) dry white wine
1 tablespoon cassis liqueur
2 ounces (60 ml) club soda
1 lemon slice

Add all ingredients to a chilled wine glass filled with ice. Stir and serve immediately.

MAKES 1 DRINK.

★ *Trivia Intermission* ★
What kind of champagne does Captain Renault recommend to Major Strasser? "Veuve Cliquot '26, a good French wine."

Classic Martini

STRASSER: What is your nationality?
RICK: I'm a drunkard.

2 ounces (60 ml) gin
2 teaspoons dry white vermouth
olive

Fill a master glass with ice. Add gin and vermouth. Stir. Strain martini into a cocktail/martini glass. Garnish with olive. Serve straight up.

Vermouth should be added to taste. For a regular martini, add 2 teaspoons vermouth; for a dry martini, add 1 teaspoon vermouth; for an extra dry martini, add only a splash of vermouth.

MAKES 1 DRINK.

"We'll Always Have Paris" Preserved Lemon Martini

2 ounces (60 ml) gin
1 teaspoon dry white vermouth
1 slice Preserved Lemon (see p. 17)

Prepare the same way as the Classic Martini, but substitute one slice of preserved lemon for the olive.

MAKES 1 DRINK.

Moroccan Mint Brandy

2 ounces (60 ml) Cointreau (or
orange-flavored brandy)
1 tablespoon Mint Syrup (see below)
fresh mint sprig

Stir together brandy and mint syrup. Serve over ice in a lowball or cordial glass. Garnish with mint sprig.

MAKES 1 DRINK.

Mint Syrup

4 cups (1 liter) water
1 cup (200 g) granulated sugar
rind of 2 oranges, in large pieces
rind of 2 lemons, in large pieces
1 vanilla bean, split and scraped
4 sprigs fresh mint

Combine all ingredients in medium saucepan. Bring to boil over medium high heat. Remove from heat when syrup reaches boil. Strain and cool. Store in refrigerator until ready to use.

MAKES 4 CUPS (1 LITER) SYRUP.

Use Mint Syrup for Blue Parrot Mint Citrus Cooler (p. 13), Minted Citrus Salad (p. 35), and Moroccan Mint Brandy (p. 8).

Rick's Whiskey Cocktail

*RICK: Tell me, who was it you left me for? Was it
Laszlo or were there others in between? Or
aren't you the kind that tells?*

1/2 teaspoon granulated sugar
water to dissolve sugar
2 ounces (60 ml) bourbon or rye whiskey*
1 to 2 drops bitters
1/2 teaspoon almond extract
whole coffee bean

At the bottom of a lowball or old-fashioned glass, add sugar and just enough water to dissolve sugar. Stir and fill with ice. In a separate master glass, add ice, whiskey, bitters, and almond extract. Stir and strain into old-fashioned glass. Garnish with coffee bean and serve.

MAKES 1 DRINK.

Señor Ferrari's Iced Almond Coffee

14 ounces (420 ml) freshly brewed coffee
1 1/2 ounces (45 ml) amaretto (almond liqueur)
unsweetened heavy whipped cream
cinnamon

Chill brewed coffee until cold. Prepare whipped cream.
Pour coffee into 2 tall glasses filled with ice. Add amaretto.
Stir. Top with whipped cream and sprinkle with cinnamon.

For a non-alcoholic version, substitute 2 teaspoons almond
extract for the amaretto.

MAKES 2 DRINKS.

After-Hours Cognac Cappuccino

RENAULT: And we have a curfew here in Casablanca.
It would never do for the Chief of Police to be
found drinking after hours and have to fine
himself.

1 ounce (30 ml) cognac
1 tablespoon honey
6 ounces (180 ml) cappuccino or
regular coffee with milk
cocoa powder

Add cognac and honey to prepared cappuccino. Sprinkle
with cocoa powder and serve immediately.

MAKES 1 DRINK.

Free France Citrus Cocktail

1 1/2 ounces (45 ml) gin
2 teaspoons Pernod or Ricard
5 ounces (150 ml) orange juice, freshly squeezed
lime wedge

Combine ingredients in a chilled glass filled with ice.
Garnish with lime wedge. Serve.

MAKES 1 DRINK.

Sacha's Lemon Vodka Fizz

3 ounces (90 ml) lemon juice, freshly squeezed
2 teaspoons granulated sugar
1 1/2 ounces (45 ml) vodka
4 ounces (120 ml) club soda
lemon peel

Combine lemon juice and sugar in a chilled highball glass;
stir to dissolve. Fill glass with ice. Add vodka and club
soda. Garnish with lemon peel and serve immediately.

MAKES 1 DRINK.

★ Trivia Time Out ★

What are the various drinks that Victor Laszlo has
at Rick's? Cointreau, champagne cocktail, cognac,
and whiskey.

Berger's Iced Mint Tea

1 1/2 tablespoons (4 tea bags) green Chinese tea
4 cups (1 liter) boiling water
1 orange, thinly sliced
1 lemon, thinly sliced
3/4 cup (150 g) granulated sugar
8 sprigs fresh mint
mint leaves

Place tea leaves or tea bags in a teapot with boiling water. Let tea steep for 5 minutes. While steeping, slice oranges and lemons and place at the bottom of a heat-resistant pitcher. Pour, or if using loose tea, strain tea into pitcher. Stir in sugar and mint leaves. Chill for at least 1 hour. Serve in tall glasses filled with ice. Garnish with mint leaves.

Moroccan tea is very sweet and minty. Decrease sugar and mint according to taste.

MAKES 4 DRINKS.

Berry Yogurt Frappe

8 ounces (227 g) plain yogurt
4 ounces (114 g) mixed berries
2 tablespoons honey
2 tablespoons orange juice, freshly squeezed
2 mint sprigs

Puree berries in a food processor or blender. Add remaining ingredients to berries. Blend until mixed. Serve immediately. Garnish with mint sprig.

Makes 2 drinks.

Blue Parrot Mint Citrus Cooler

1 1/2 cups (360 ml) orange juice, freshly squeezed
3/4 cup (180 ml) lemon juice, freshly squeezed
1 cup (240 ml) grapefruit juice, freshly squeezed
1 1/2 cups (360 ml) Mint Syrup (see p. 8)
4 mint sprigs
4 lime slices

Mix all ingredients in a pitcher. Chill and serve over crushed ice in tall glasses. Garnish with mint sprigs and lime slices.

This is a refreshing, not too sweet, mint citrus drink. If you prefer a sweeter drink, add sugar to taste.

Makes 4 drinks.

Café Americain Almonds

1/2 ounce (14 g) unsalted butter, melted
1 teaspoon ground cumin
1/2 teaspoon cayenne pepper
1/2 teaspoon salt
1 cup (160 g) whole natural almonds

Preheat oven to 375°F (191°C). Combine melted butter with cumin, cayenne, and salt in a medium bowl. Toss almonds in mixture, coating well. Place on baking sheet. Bake 8 minutes or until almonds are lightly toasted, turning almonds occasionally. Cool.

MAKES 1 CUP (160 G). RECIPE CAN EASILY BE DOUBLED.

Emil's Aromatic Herb Mix

4 garlic cloves, chopped
2 tablespoons parsley, chopped
2 tablespoons coriander leaves, chopped
1 teaspoon dried marjoram
1 teaspoon salt
1/2 teaspoon freshly ground black pepper
1/8 teaspoon cayenne pepper
1/2 teaspoon dried thyme
1/2 teaspoon saffron threads

Mix all ingredients in a small bowl. Store in refrigerator in airtight container until ready to use. Keeps 2 to 3 days.

Use Emil's Aromatic Herb Mix in Spiced Green Olives (p. 15), Swordfish Brochettes (p. 23), and Louis's Sure-Bet Potato Salad (p.34)

Abdul's Secret Spice Mix

1/2 teaspoon ground cinnamon
1 teaspoon ground turmeric
1 teaspoon ground cumin
1 teaspoon ground coriander
1/4 teaspoon freshly ground black pepper
1/4 teaspoon ground nutmeg
1/2 teaspoon red pepper flakes
1 teaspoon saffron threads
1 teaspoon salt

Mix all spices in a small bowl.

Use to season Marinated Black Olives (p. 16), Goat-Cheese Purses (p. 28), and Couscous Marocain (p. 25).

Spiced Green Olives

16 ounces (454 g) green olives
3 tablespoons olive oil
1 teaspoon honey
1 recipe Emil's Aromatic Herb Mix (see p. 14)

Combine all ingredients in a medium bowl. Cover and refrigerate overnight. Serve with cocktails. Keeps 1 week in refrigerator.

MAKES 1 POUND (454 G) OLIVES.

Marinated Black Olives

*RENAULT: And what in heaven's name brought you to
    Casablanca?*
RICK: My health. I came to Casablanca for the waters.
RENAULT: Waters? What waters? We're in the desert.
RICK: I was misinformed.

16 ounces (454 g) black niçoise olives in brine
2 teaspoons Abdul's Secret Spice Mix (see p. 15)
2 tablespoons Preserved Lemon rind,
finely chopped (see p. 17)
1 teaspoon red pepper flakes

Mix all ingredients in a medium bowl. Allow to marinate
overnight or longer in refrigerator. Keeps 2 weeks.
(Freshly grated lemon rind may be substituted for preserved lemons.)

MAKES 1 POUND (454 G).

Sugar-Preserved Lemons

4 small lemons
2 cups (400 g) granulated sugar

Slice lemons as thinly as possible. In a 1-quart (1 liter)
jar, layer lemons alternately with sugar to fill jar. Seal
jar with airtight lid. By the following day, the mixture
should have produced enough liquid to cover the lemons.
If not, add additional sugar. Do not add water. Let sit
in cool, dry spot for 2 weeks. After 2 weeks lemons are
ready to use. Refrigerate at this point to store lemons up
to 6 months.

Use Sugar-Preserved Lemons in Lemon Yogurt Cake (p. 53) and "As Time Goes By" Preserved Lemon Cookies (p. 64). They may also be used to flavor butter or to sprinkle on berries, or may be substituted for plain lemon rind in other dessert recipes.

Preserved Lemons

4 small lemons
2 cups (400 g) salt

Follow the previous recipe, using salt instead of sugar. Also, rather than slicing the lemons, poke holes with a sharp knife all around the middle of the lemons. These are a traditional Moroccan seasoning which can be used to add flavor to many dishes, including soups and stews.

Use in "We'll Always Have Paris" Preserved Lemon Martini (p. 8) and Marinated Black Olives (p. 16).

KEBABS AND OTHER HORS D'OEUVRES

*"Oh, waiter. I'll be expecting some people."
"Champagne and a tin of caviar."*

Carl's Coriander Shrimp Kebabs

24 medium shrimp, shelled and cleaned
1/2 cup (120 ml) olive oil
1/3 cup (80 ml) lemon juice
1 teaspoon salt
1/2 teaspoon freshly ground black pepper
2 teaspoons dried marjoram
4 garlic cloves, chopped
6 sprigs fresh coriander, coarsely chopped

Mix all ingredients in medium bowl. Let shrimp marinate several hours or refrigerate overnight. Spear 3 shrimp on each skewer. Broil or grill 2 minutes on each side, until shrimp are cooked through.

MAKES 8 KEBABS.

Major Strasser's Ground Lamb Kebabs

STRASSER: Very well, Herr Laszlo, we will not mince words. You are an escaped prisoner of the Reich.

1 1/2 pounds (681 g) ground lamb
1 teaspoon ground cumin
1 teaspoon cinnamon
2 tablespoons fresh coriander leaves, chopped
1 medium onion, finely chopped
2 garlic cloves, minced
1/2 teaspoon salt
1/4 teaspoon freshly ground black pepper
1/3 teaspoon cayenne pepper
1/4 cup (30 g) ground almonds

Mix all ingredients in a medium bowl until well blended. Shape mixture into 1 1/2-inch (38 mm) balls. Put 3 meatballs onto each skewer. Bake at 350°F (177°C) for about 10 minutes, or grill over medium flame, until meat is cooked. Serve with Yogurt Mint Dipping Sauce (see p. 21) and warm pita bread. (Note: If wooden skewers are used, soak them in cold water for 1 hour before cooking.)

MAKES 10 KEBABS (30 MEATBALLS).

Yogurt Mint Dipping Sauce

8 ounces (227 g) plain nonfat yogurt
1 tablespoon fresh mint leaves, chopped
2 teaspoons honey
1/4 teaspoon salt

Stir ingredients together in a small bowl.

Serve as a dipping sauce for Major Strasser's Ground Lamb Kebabs (p. 20), Yvonne's Spicy Potato Balls (p. 26), and Emil's Chick-Pea Fritters (p. 31).

Chicken Apricot Kebabs

*2 whole chicken breasts, cut into
1 1/2-inch (38 mm) pieces
3 small cloves garlic, chopped
1 cinnamon stick
1 teaspoon salt
several grinds pepper
1/4 teaspoon ground ginger
1/4 teaspoon ground cinnamon
juice of 1 orange (scant 1/4 cup)
1 tablespoon honey
1 tablespoon olive oil
8 to 9 fresh apricots, halved*

GLAZE:
*2 tablespoons honey
1 tablespoon orange juice
1 tablespoon lemon juice*

Put chicken pieces in a medium bowl. Add next 9 ingredients and mix thoroughly. Cover with plastic wrap and let marinate at least 2 hours or refrigerate overnight. Thread chicken and apricot halves on skewers alternating 2 chicken pieces with 1 apricot half. Grill over charcoal or on a gas grill set to low for about 15 minutes, turning once and basting with marinade. Just before chicken is ready to come off grill, brush with glaze. Remove from grill. (Note: If wooden skewers are used, soak them in cold water for 1 hour before cooking.)

For glaze, combine honey and juices in a small saucepan and bring to a boil. Cool.

MAKES 6 KEBABS.

Swordfish Brochettes

*1 1/2 pounds (681 g) swordfish, trimmed and cut into
1 1/2-inch (38 mm) cubes
1/4 cup (60 ml) olive oil
2 teaspoons honey
1 tablespoon lime juice
1/2 recipe of Emil's Aromatic Herb Mix (see p. 14)
2 red peppers, cut into 1 1/2-inch cubes*

Combine olive oil, honey, lime juice, and herbs. Let swordfish cubes marinate in mixture for 2 hours at room temperature or overnight in refrigerator. Thread four pieces of
fish and three pieces of red pepper on each skewer. Grill or
broil 2 to 3 minutes on each side, brushing with the marinade. Do not overcook. (Note: If wooden skewers are used,
soak them in cold water for 1 hour before cooking.)

MAKES ABOUT 8 KEBABS.

★ Casablanca Charades ★

*Play charades using only movies that Casablanca actors
appeared in. If you have a group of real pros, guess the
movie name and the actor who was in it. Here are some sug-
gestions: Humphrey Bogart—The Oklahoma Kid, The
Return of Dr. X, High Sierra, The Maltese Falcon; Ingrid
Bergman—Intermezzo, Rage in Heaven, For Whom the Bell
Tolls, Government Girl; Paul Henreid—Now, Voyager, Joan
of Paris; Claude Rains—The Adventures of Robin Hood, The
Invisible Man, Notorious; Conrad Veidt—The Cabinet of Dr.
Caligari, The Thief of Bagdad; Peter Lorre—M, Arsenic and
Old Lace, Beat the Devil; Dooley Wilson—My Favorite
Blonde, Night in New Orleans; S. Z. Sakall—Yankee Doodle
Dandy, Ball of Fire.*

"Vive La France" Vegetable Kebabs

1 yellow pepper, cut into 1 1/2-inch (38 mm) cubes
1 sweet red pepper, cut into 1 1/2-inch (38 mm) cubes
2 small zucchini, sliced 1/2 inch (13 mm) thick
1 medium eggplant, cut into 1 1/2-inch (38 mm) cubes
2 tablespoons honey
1/4 cup (60 ml) vinegar
1/2 cup (120 ml) olive oil
1 teaspoon salt
1/4 teaspoon freshly ground black pepper
2 teaspoons ground coriander

Mix vegetables with remaining ingredients in a large bowl. Let marinate 4 hours at room temperature, basting vegetables with marinade every 30 minutes. Thread vegetables on skewers. Grill or broil vegetables about 3 minutes on each side, until vegetables begin to brown. Serve with remaining marinade as a dipping sauce. (Note: If wooden skewers are used, soak them in cold water for 1 hour before cooking.)

MAKES 10 KEBABS.

Couscous Marocain

16 ounces (454 g) couscous
1 recipe Abdul's Secret Spice Mix (see p. 15)
1 cup (284 g) raisins
1 19-ounce (540 g) can chick peas
2 cloves garlic, chopped
1 tablespoon fresh coriander, chopped
1 large tomato, diced
1 red onion, diced
juice of 1 lemon
juice of 1 orange
4 tablespoons olive oil
2 cups (480 ml) unsalted chicken broth or water

Place dried couscous in a fine strainer. Pour cold water over the couscous until it is completely wet. Let drain for 30 seconds. Spread couscous on a cookie sheet and cover with a damp towel. Let sit for 30 minutes. Then take couscous and pour it into a large bowl. Separate it into grains with your fingers. Mix in all remaining ingredients. Up until this point couscous can be prepared ahead and refrigerated up to 3 days. When ready to serve, place couscous in a large ovenproof dish with water or chicken broth. Bake covered at 400°F (204°C) until couscous is hot and all the liquid is absorbed (about 20 minutes). Couscous goes well with kebabs.

MAKES 6 TO 8 SERVINGS.

Yvonne's Spicy Potato Balls

Yvonne: Where were you last night?
Rick: That's so long ago, I don't remember.
Yvonne: Will I see you tonight?
Rick: I never make plans that far ahead.

1 cup (200 g) mashed potatoes
¹/₂ cup (8 sprigs) fresh mint, chopped
1 teaspoon salt
¹/₂ teaspoon cayenne pepper
¹/₂ teaspoon ground coriander
¹/₂ cup (50 g) seasoned dry bread crumbs
1 egg, beaten
vegetable oil for frying
1 recipe Yogurt Mint Dipping Sauce (see p. 21)

Combine mashed potatoes, chopped mint, salt, cayenne, and coriander in a medium bowl. Shape into balls, using 1 tablespoon of the mixture for each one. Roll balls in bread crumbs, then into egg. Roll again in crumbs. Heat oil over medium heat in a deep saucepan. Cook potato balls about 1 minute until browned and crisp. Drain well. Serve with Yogurt Mint Dipping Sauce.

MAKES 16 BALLS.

Moor's Bisteeya

2 tablespoons olive oil
1 medium onion, chopped
1 pound (454 g) ground lamb or beef
2 cloves garlic, minced
3 tablespoons parsley, chopped

1 teaspoon salt
1/4 teaspoon freshly ground black pepper
3/4 teaspoon ground cinnamon
2 eggs, lightly beaten
7 sheets filo pastry
2 ounces (57 g) unsalted butter, melted
1/2 cup (40 g) blanched almonds, sliced
2 teaspoons confectioners' sugar

Preheat oven to 400°F (204°C). To prepare filling: Heat oil in a large skillet. Saute onion over medium heat until tender. Add ground meat, garlic, parsley, salt, pepper, and 1/4 teaspoon cinnamon. Continue to cook over medium high heat until lamb is browned. Remove from heat. Stir in eggs. Set aside.

Lay first sheet of filo onto baking sheet. The standard size is 9 inches (23 cm) by 13 inches (33 cm), but filo can be trimmed to fit the sheet if necessary). Brush pastry lightly with butter. Lay second sheet on first one. Brush second sheet with butter. Place a third sheet of filo on the sheet pan. Brush with butter. Sprinkle 1/4 teaspoon cinnamon and 1/4 cup almonds over pastry. Spread filling evenly over pastry, leaving a 1-inch (25 mm) border of filo around the edges. Lay the fourth sheet of pastry over this; butter lightly. Repeat with fifth and sixth sheets. After buttering sixth sheet, sprinkle with 1/4 teaspoon cinnamon, 1/4 cup (20 g) almonds, and the confectioners' sugar. Top with remaining sheet of filo. Butter lightly. Bake 20 to 25 minutes until filo is golden and crisp. Cut into 24 squares and serve immediately.

MAKES 24 SQUARES.

Goat-Cheese Purses

Dark European: I have to warn you, sir. I beseech you.
(The tourist laughs nervously. The dark European picks
his pocket.)
Dark European: This is a dangerous place, full of vul-
tures. Vultures everywhere! Thanks for everything.

11 ounces (312 g) goat cheese
4 ounces (114 g) cream cheese
2 teaspoons Abdul's Secret Spice Mix (see p.15)
$1/2$ teaspoon turmeric
1 sweet red pepper, roasted (see note below) and
chopped
10 sheets filo pastry
4 ounces (114 g) unsalted butter, melted
$3/4$ cup (80 g) grated parmesan cheese

Combine goat cheese, cream cheese, spice mix, turmeric,
and red pepper in a medium bowl. Lay 1 sheet of filo
pastry on counter. Brush lightly with melted butter and
sprinkle with 1 teaspoon parmesan cheese. Lay second
sheet onto first sheet. Repeat with butter and parmesan
cheese. Cut filo into 6 strips, each 2 inches (3 cm) wide by
12 inches (30 cm) long. At the top of each strip place one
rounded teaspoon of filling. Fold filo to make a triangle
in the way you would fold an American flag. Brush with
butter at edge to seal. Continue until all filling is used,
using 2 filo leaves each time. When ready to serve, preheat oven to 400°F (204°C). Brush triangles with butter
and sprinkle with remaining parmesan cheese. Bake 10
minutes until triangles are golden. Let cool 3 minutes.

These may be made ahead and frozen. When ready to
use, bake still-frozen packets for 12 minutes.

NOTE: To roast red pepper, broil or grill pepper until skin is charred. Remove from heat. Peel skin. Trim pepper and remove seeds.

MAKES 30 PACKETS.

Tuna Tapenade

1 6 1/8-ounce (175 g) can tuna
1 6-ounce (170 g) can black olives, pitted
4 anchovy fillets
2 tablespoons capers
2 tablespoons olive oil
2 teaspoons dijon mustard
1 large garlic clove
toasted pita triangles

Combine tuna, olives, anchovies, capers, olive oil, mustard, and garlic in food processor or blender. Blend until smooth. Serve tapenade with toasted pita triangles.

MAKES 1 1/3 CUPS (320 ML).

Ugarte's Tangy Chicken Wings

3 pounds (1362 g) chicken wings
1/2 cup (120 g) dijon mustard
3/4 cup (225 g) honey
1 tablespoon grated fresh ginger root
1 tablespoon fresh coriander leaves, chopped
3 tablespoons lemon juice
1 teaspoon salt
1/4 teaspoon freshly ground black pepper
2 cloves garlic, finely chopped
2 tablespoons harissa (see below)

Mix all ingredients in a large bowl. Marinate chicken for 2 to 3 hours in refrigerator. Grill chicken wings on charcoal or gas grill until cooked, basting frequently with marinade. Instead of grilling, wings can also be baked. To bake, preheat oven to 400°F (204°C). Bake wings on cookie sheet or broiler pan for 10 minutes. Turn wings and baste with marinade. Broil for about 3 minutes until wings are browned.

Harissa is a spicy red pepper paste. If not available, substitute 2 to 3 tablespoons tomato paste mixed with 1/2 teaspoon cayenne pepper. Spice range: 1 tablespoon harissa = mild; 2 tablespoons harissa = medium; 3 tablespoons harissa = very hot.

MAKES 25 WINGS.

Emil's Chick-Pea Fritters

1 19-ounce (540 g) can chick-peas
1 egg
3 teaspoons Abdul's Secret Spice Mix (see p. 15)
1/2 cup (65 g) flour
1 quart (1 liter) vegetable oil
salt and cayenne pepper to taste

Puree chick-peas in a food processor or blender. Add egg and spice mixture. Continue to blend until just incorporated. Coat hands with flour. Shape mixture into 1 1/2-inch (38 mm) fritters, coating hands with flour after each one. Place fritters on a cookie sheet lined with wax paper or parchment. Cover and chill until ready to fry, at least 15 minutes. Heat oil to 375°F (191°C). Fry chick-pea fritters about 1 minute until golden brown. Drain on paper towels. Sprinkle with salt and cayenne pepper if desired. Serve immediately, with Yogurt Mint Dipping Sauce (p. 21).

MAKES 40 FRITTERS.

SWEET AND SAVORY SALADS

*"The problems of three
little people don't amount
to a hill of beans in this
crazy world."*

Louis's Sure-Bet Potato Salad

*RICK: He (Laszlo) escaped from a concentration camp
and the Nazis have been chasing him all over Europe.*
RENAULT: This is the end of the chase.
RICK: Twenty thousand francs says it isn't.
RENAULT: Is that a serious offer?
RICK: I just paid out twenty. I'd like to get it back.
RENAULT: Make it ten. I am only a poor corrupt official.

*2 pounds (908 g) red potatoes, cut into bite-size
chunks*
2 medium celery stalks, sliced
1 medium carrot, grated
3 tablespoons olive oil
2 tablespoons lemon juice
1 recipe Emil's Aromatic Herb Mix (see p. 14)

Place potatoes in a medium saucepan with enough water
to cover. Bring to a boil over high heat. Reduce heat to
low. Cover and simmer 20 minutes or until potatoes are
tender. Drain. While potatoes are cooking, combine
remaining ingredients in a large bowl. Toss with potatoes
and mix well.

MAKES 6 SERVINGS.

Casablanca Couscous Salad

1 2/3 cups (400 ml) chicken broth
1 cup (140 g) couscous
1 medium tomato, diced
1 medium cucumber, peeled and diced
1 medium scallion, sliced
1/4 cup (30 g) pignolia nuts

1/4 cup (29 g) golden raisins or currants
1/4 cup (60 ml) lemon juice
1/4 cup (60 ml) olive oil
3 tablespoons fresh mint, chopped
2 tablespoons fresh parsley, chopped
3/4 teaspoon salt
1/4 teaspoon ground black pepper

Bring chicken broth to boil in a small saucepan over high heat. Add couscous. Reduce heat to low. Cover and simmer 3 to 5 minutes until liquid is absorbed. Remove from heat. Cool to room temperature. Meanwhile, combine remaining ingredients in a large bowl. Toss with couscous and mix well.

MAKES 4 SERVINGS.

Minted Citrus Salad

1/2 pound (227 g) pitted cherries
5 oranges, peeled and sectioned
3 pink grapefruits, peeled and sectioned
1 1/2 cups (360 ml) Mint Syrup (see p. 8)
fresh mint sprigs

Mix fruit together in a medium serving bowl. Pour mint syrup over fruit and allow to marinate in refrigerator overnight. Serve fruit with syrup. Garnish with fresh mint sprigs.

MAKES 4 SERVINGS.

Exit-Visa Eggplant Salad

RENAULT: *Rick, there are many exit visas sold in this café,
but we know that you have never sold one. That is the
reason we permit you to remain open.*
RICK: *I thought it was because we let you win at roulette.*
RENAULT: *Er, that is another reason.*

1 large eggplant, cut into 1-inch (25 mm) cubes
$1/_3$ cup (80 ml) olive oil
1 large onion, diced
2 red or yellow bell peppers, seeded and cut into
thin strips
3 large garlic cloves, crushed
$1/_4$ cup (40 g) pitted black olives, chopped
3 tablespoons chopped parsley
$1 1/_4$ teaspoons salt
$1/_8$ teaspoon cayenne pepper

Cook eggplant cubes in hot oil in a large saucepan over
medium heat for 5 minutes, stirring occasionally. Add
diced onion. Cook an additional 5 minutes. Add peppers
and garlic. Cook 5 minutes longer, stirring occasionally,
until vegetables are tender. In a large bowl toss mixture
with olives, parsley, salt, and pepper until well mixed.
Serve warm or refrigerate to serve cold later.

MAKES 4 SERVINGS.

Laszlo's Seafood Marseillaise

1/2 pound (227 g) squid
1 teaspoon salt
2 tablespoons olive oil
1/2 pound (227 g) medium shrimp, peeled and cleaned
1/2 pound (227 g) bay scallops
1 large garlic clove, crushed
1 large tomato, diced
1/4 cup (40 g) green olives, sliced and pitted
3 tablespoons chopped parsley
2 tablespoons lemon juice
1 teaspoon ground coriander

Prepare squid by removing tentacles from body. Then cut off and discard portion of tentacles containing sac. Remove thin, transparent cartilage and all loose pieces from inside body. Using your fingers, gently scrape and pull off thin dark outer skin from squid. Rinse tentacles and body under running cold water. Slice body into 1/2-inch-thick rings (13 mm). Cut tentacles in half.

Bring 1/2 inch (13 mm) of water and 1/2 teaspoon salt to a boil in a small saucepan over high heat. Add squid and return to a boil. Reduce heat to medium and cook for 3 to 5 minutes until squid is tender and opaque. Drain well and place in a large bowl.

In a large skillet over medium-high heat, lightly brown shrimp, scallops, and garlic until tender, stirring frequently. Toss remaining ingredients with 1/2 teaspoon salt and cooked seafood in a large bowl. Mix well. Cover and refrigerate at least 2 hours to blend flavors, stirring occasionally.

MAKES 6 SERVINGS.

Courier Carrot and Beet Slaw

UGARTE: You despise me, don't you?
RICK: If I gave you any thought, I probably would.

2 pounds fresh beets or 2 16-ounce (908 g) cans whole
beets, drained
3 tablespoons olive oil
3 tablespoons lemon juice
1 small garlic clove, crushed
1/2 teaspoon ground cumin
1/2 teaspoon salt
1/2 teaspoon granulated sugar
1/4 teaspoon black pepper
4 medium carrots, peeled

Preheat oven to 400°F (204°C). If beets are large, cut each one in half. Place in foil-lined baking pan. Roast beets 45 to 60 minutes (depending on size) until they feel tender when tested with a fork. Set aside until cool enough to handle. (Skip this part if using canned beets.)

While beets are roasting, combine olive oil, lemon juice, garlic, cumin, salt, sugar, and pepper. Peel beets. Cut beets and carrots into julienne strips, either by hand or preferably in a food processor with a julienne cutting attachment. Toss with dressing until well mixed.

MAKES 6 SERVINGS.

Ugarte's Orange and Artichoke Salad

UGARTE: You know, Rick, I have many friends in Casablanca, but somehow, just because you despise me, you're the only one I trust.

2 9-ounce (510 g) packages frozen artichoke hearts
$1/_2$ cup (120 ml) orange juice
3 medium navel oranges, peeled
2 tablespoons fresh parsley, chopped
1 tablespoon olive oil
2 teaspoons grated orange peel
$1/_2$ teaspoon dried marjoram
$1/_2$ teaspoon granulated sugar
$1/_4$ teaspoon salt

Combine frozen artichoke hearts and orange juice in a medium saucepan. Bring to a boil over high heat. Reduce heat to low. Cover and simmer 5 minutes until artichokes are tender. Drain artichokes, reserving 2 tablespoons of the orange-juice liquid. Set aside and cool to room temperature. While artichokes are cooking, cut oranges in $1/_4$-inch-thick (6 mm) slices. Cut each slice in half. In medium bowl combine parsley, olive oil, grated orange peel, marjoram, sugar, and salt. Toss with orange slices, artichokes, and reserved liquid.

MAKES 6 SERVINGS.

Kasbah Chick-Pea Salad

2 tablespoons olive oil
1 medium red onion, diced
2 teaspoons ground cumin
1 medium cucumber, peeled
1 19-ounce (540 g) can chick-peas (garbanzo beans),
drained and rinsed
2 tablespoons lemon juice
3/4 teaspoon salt

Cook red onion in hot oil in a small over medium heat for
about 3 minutes or until crisp-tender. Stir in cumin.
Cook 1 minute longer. Cut cucumber in half lengthwise.
Cut halves into 1/4-inch-thick (6 mm) slices. Toss cucumber, chick-peas, lemon juice, salt, and onion mixture in a
medium bowl. Mix well.

MAKES 4 SERVINGS.

Last-Plane-Out Lentil and Lamb Salad

RICK: If that plane leaves the ground and you're
not with him, you'll regret it.
Ilsa: No.
RICK: Maybe not today, maybe not tomorrow, but
soon, and for the rest of your life.

1 pound (454 g) lamb, cut into 3/4-inch (19 mm) chunks
2 tablespoons olive oil
3 medium carrots, peeled and thinly sliced
1 medium onion, diced
2 large garlic cloves, chopped
2 cups (480 ml) water
1 cup (220 g) dried green lentils, rinsed and drained

1 1/2 teaspoons salt
1 teaspoon ground cumin seed
1/4 teaspoon crushed red pepper

Cook lamb in oil in a large saucepan over medium-high heat until well browned on all sides, stirring frequently. Remove to bowl. Cook carrots, onion, and garlic in the drippings remaining in the saucepan over medium heat for 5 minutes, stirring occasionally. Add water, lentils, salt, cumin, crushed red pepper, and lamb. Bring to a boil over high heat. Reduce heat to low. Cover and simmer 45 minutes or until lentils and lamb are tender, stirring occasionally.

MAKES 6 SERVINGS.

Carrot Salad Vichy

RICK: Louis, I think this is the beginning of a beautiful friendship.

1 ounce (28 g) unsalted butter
1 pound (454 g) baby carrots, peeled
2 teaspoons granulated sugar
2 tablespoons water
1 tablespoon cider vinegar
1/2 teaspoon salt
2 tablespoons fresh coriander, chopped

Melt butter over medium heat in a medium saucepan. Add baby carrots and sugar. Stir to coat well. Stir in water, vinegar, and salt. Bring to a boil over high heat. Reduce heat to low. Cover and simmer 15 minutes or until carrots are tender. Stir in coriander. Serve warm or cool to room temperature.

MAKES 4 SERVINGS.

TREASURED
DESSERTS

*"The leading banker in
Amsterdam is now the
pastry chef in our kitchen."*

"Play It" Plum Parfait

ILSA: Play it once, Sam, for old time's sake.
SAM: I don't know what you mean, Miss Ilsa.
ILSA: Play it, Sam. Play "As Time Goes By."

1 ounce (28 g) unsalted butter
2 tablespoons honey
1 cup (80 g) sliced almonds
1/4 teaspoon ground ginger
1/4 teaspoon cinnamon
2 large plums
3 tablespoons orange juice
2 tablespoons brown sugar
1 cinnamon stick
1 2-inch (50 mm) piece fresh ginger, peeled
1 pint (454 g) vanilla ice cream

Melt butter in medium saucepan or frying pan. Add honey and stir, then add almonds. Cook until almonds start to brown and honey starts to caramelize slightly. Remove from heat and add ground ginger and cinnamon. Let cool. Chop coarsely.

Cut plums into 1/2-inch (13 mm) slices. Put into a small saucepan. Add orange juice, brown sugar, cinnamon stick, and fresh ginger. Cook over low heat about 4 or 5 minutes, or until plums are soft but not mushy. Cool.

Using 4 tall clear glasses, alternate scoops of ice cream, almond mixture, and plums until glasses are filled. Garnish with fresh mint if desired.

MAKES 4 PARFAITS.

Melon with Frozen Lemon Cream

³/₄ cup plus 1 tablespoon (200 ml) fresh lemon juice
¹/₂ cup plus 1 tablespoon (105 g) granulated sugar
³/₄ cup (180 ml) heavy cream
2 medium cantaloupes
1 small honeydew melon
4 tablespoons fresh mint, chopped
mint sprigs

Heat ³/₄ cup (185 ml) lemon juice in small non-aluminum saucepan. Stir in ¹/₂ cup (100 g) sugar until dissolved. Remove from heat; let cool completely. Stir in heavy cream. Pour into bowl and place in freezer for at least 1 hour, until frozen but still soft. Cut cantaloupes in half. Scoop out seeds. With a spoon remove about half of flesh from fruit. Chop coarsely. Peel honeydew with a serrated knife; remove seeds. Coarsely chop and add to the chopped cantaloupe. Add chopped mint, remaining tablespoon of lemon juice, and remaining tablespoon of sugar. Spoon into four melon halves. Top each with a scoop of frozen lemon cream. Garnish with mint sprigs.

MAKES 4 SERVINGS.

Couscous Soufflé with Date Ice Cream

1/2 vanilla bean
1 cup (240 ml) milk
1/3 cup couscous (47 g)
pinch of salt
2 tablespoons honey
1 tablespoon unsalted butter
grated rind of 1 medium orange
2 tablespoons orange juice
1 teaspoon orange flower water
3 eggs, separated
2 tablespoons granulated sugar

ICE CREAM:
1 pint (454 g) vanilla ice cream
1 cup (227 g) dates, coarsely chopped

Preheat oven to 375°F (191°C). Grease a 1 1/2-quart (1 1/2 liter) soufflé dish. Scrape seeds from vanilla bean into milk. Bring milk to a boil. Lower heat and stir in couscous, then salt, honey, and butter. Cook about 3 minutes, or until liquid is 3/4 absorbed. Transfer mixture to a medium bowl. Stir in orange rind, orange juice, flower water, and egg yolks. Put whites into mixing bowl. Beat at medium speed until frothy. Slowly add sugar while beating. Continue to beat until stiff but not dry. Fold 1/4 of the whites into the couscous mixture, then fold in remaining whites. Turn into soufflé dish and bake about 18 minutes. Soufflé will brown lightly, but the very center should still be soft. Serve immediately with a scoop of date ice cream.

To make ice cream, first chop dates coarsely. Put them into a medium bowl. Scoop ice cream into bowl. Mix together using a wooden spoon or spatula. Cover with plastic wrap and return to freezer.

MAKES 6 SERVINGS.

Rick and Ilsa's Apricot Pistachio Cake

ILSA: Was that cannon fire, or is it my heart pounding?

1/2 pound (277 g) dried apricots
4 ounces (114 g) unsalted butter
1 cup (200 g) granulated sugar
2 eggs
1 teaspoon vanilla extract
3 tablespoons sour cream
1 1/2 cups (195 g) flour
1 teaspoon baking soda
1/2 teaspoon salt
2/3 cup (85 g) pistachio nuts, chopped

Preheat oven to 350°F (177°C). Grease and flour a (5 cup or 1 1/4 liter capacity) loaf pan. Put apricots in a pot with 2 cups (480 ml) of water. Bring to boil over medium heat. Gently simmer for 1/2 hour or until apricots are soft. Drain apricots and puree in food processor or blender. Cream butter and sugar until light and fluffy. Add eggs one at a time, beating after each addition. Add vanilla, apricot puree, and sour cream. Mix until smooth. Mix flour, baking soda, salt, and nuts in a separate bowl. Fold dry ingredients into batter with spatula. Bake 40 minutes or until toothpick comes out clean. Unmold cake after 5 minutes. Cool.

MAKES 1 LOAF.

Jan's Sesame Bread

3 cups (720 ml) water
4 tea bags
1 pound or 2 cups (454 g) pitted prunes
3/4 cup (180 ml) vegetable oil
1 cup (200 g) granulated sugar
5 eggs
12 ounces (350 g) plain yogurt
4 cups (520 g) flour
1/2 teaspoon salt
1 tablespoon baking soda
1/2 cup (70 g) toasted sesame seeds

Preheat oven to 350°F (177°C). Grease and flour 2 medium loaf pans (5 cup or 1 1/4 liter capacity). Bring water to a boil in a medium saucepan. Remove from heat. Add tea bags and prunes. Let steep for 15 minutes. Remove tea bags. Drain prunes and cut into 1-inch (25 mm) pieces. In a large mixing bowl, beat oil and sugar at medium speed. Add eggs one at a time, beating well after each addition. Add yogurt and prunes. Mix well. Mix flour, baking soda, salt, and sesame seeds in a separate bowl. Fold dry ingredients into batter until just incorporated. Pour batter into prepared loaf pans. Bake at 350°F (177°C) for about 40 minutes, until cake tester or toothpick comes out clean. Let cool in pans 5 minutes. Unmold and let cool. Serve with Annina's Honey Butter.

MAKES 2 LOAVES.

ANNINA'S HONEY BUTTER
8 ounces (227 g) unsalted butter, softened
2 tablespoons honey

Cream honey and butter until smooth. Scrape into bowl and refrigerate until ready to use.

Serve with Jan's Sesame Bread.

Heinrich's Honey-Roasted Pears

*STRASSER: We know that every French province in
Africa is honeycombed with traitors...*

4 pears, cored and halved
1 ounce (28 g) unsalted butter
2 tablespoons honey
1 cinnamon stick, broken into 8 pieces
4 pieces star anise, broken in half
juice of 1/2 lemon
2 tablespoons anise-flavored liqueur
3/4 cup (180 ml) heavy cream
2 tablespoons sour cream

Preheat oven to 400°F (204°C). Grease a shallow baking dish. Arrange pears cut-side up in dish. Dot with butter. Drizzle with honey. Put a piece of cinnamon stick and star anise in each pear half. Drizzle with lemon juice and anise liqueur. Bake until pears are soft but not mushy, about 20 to 30 minutes (depending on ripeness of pears). Remove pears from baking dish with slotted spoon or spatula and place on serving dish. Pour juices from dish into a small bowl. Refrigerate until cool. Put heavy cream and sour cream into a medium mixing bowl. Beat until cream begins to thicken. Pour 1/4 cup (60 ml) cool pear syrup into cream and beat until soft peaks form. Serve pears with a dollop of this whipped cream. Garnish with star anise.

MAKES 8 PEAR HALVES.

Corina's Banana Fritters

1/4 cup (20 g) cornstarch
1/4 cup (33 g) flour
pinch salt
3 tablespoons toasted sesame seeds
1 egg, separated
1/2 cup (120 ml) beer
6 medium bananas
confectioners' sugar for dusting
1 recipe Orange Sauce

Make fritter batter 1 to 4 hours in advance. Place cornstarch, flour, salt, and 2 tablespoons sesame seeds in a medium bowl. Make a small well in the center of flour mixture. Drop egg yolk into well. Mix together with whisk, while slowly pouring in beer. When beer is fully incorporated, cover bowl and refrigerate 1/2 hour. When batter has chilled, beat egg white at medium speed until soft peaks form. Continue to beat on high speed a few more seconds. Whites will still be slightly soft but should not be dry. Stir egg white gently into batter. Heat oil in medium saucepan to 375°F (191°C); use a deep-fry or candy thermometer to check temperature. Peel and halve bananas lengthwise. Cut each half into 3 equal pieces. When oil is ready, drop banana pieces, four at a time, into batter. Coat pieces completely with batter. Drop coated bananas into hot oil. Fry for about 1 minute, until bananas are golden. Remove from oil with slotted spoon. Drain on paper towels. Sprinkle with confectioners' sugar and remaining sesame seeds. Serve immediately with Orange Sauce.

MAKES 6 SERVINGS.

ORANGE SAUCE
1 cup (240 ml) orange juice, freshly squeezed
2 tablespoons granulated sugar
1 tablespoon rum (optional)

Place orange juice and sugar in a small non-aluminum saucepan. Bring to boil and let reduce to $1/4$ cup (60 ml) liquid (10 to 15 minutes). Remove from heat. Stir in rum. Refrigerate until ready to serve.

Mango Yogurt

3 large ripe mangoes
8 ounces (227 g) plain yogurt

Peel mangoes and cut flesh from the pits. Puree the fruit in a food processor or blender until smooth. Add yogurt and blend. Spoon into 4 wineglasses. Chill for at least 1 hour. Serve with Preserved Lemon Cookies (see p. 64).

MAKES 4 SERVINGS.

Black-Market Honey Chocolate Mousse

4 eggs, separated
2 teaspoons instant coffee
1/3 cup (100 g) honey
4 ounces (114 g) bittersweet or semi-sweet chocolate
2 tablespoons granulated sugar
4 tablespoons toasted pine nuts

Put yolks, instant coffee, and honey into a mixing bowl over saucepan of gently simmering water. Whisk yolk mixture and heat until it becomes hot to the touch. Remove mixture from heat and beat with electric mixer until very thick. Meanwhile, melt chocolate in a small bowl over saucepan of gently simmering water. Set chocolate aside. Stir egg yolk mixture into warm (not hot) melted chocolate. Beat egg whites with electric mixer until soft peaks form. Gradually add sugar while continuing to beat on low speed. Increase speed to high and beat until stiff peaks form. Whisk 1/4 of whites into chocolate yolk mixture. Fold remaining whites into the mixture. Scrape into serving bowl. Sprinkle with toasted pine nuts. Refrigerate at least 1 hour before serving.

MAKES 4 SERVINGS.

Lemon Yogurt Cake

2 1/4 cups (292 g) flour
1 teaspoon baking powder
1 teaspoon baking soda
1/4 teaspoon salt
4 ounces (114 g) unsalted butter
3/4 cup (150 g) granulated sugar
2 eggs
8 ounces (227 g) plain yogurt
2 tablespoons Sugar-Preserved Lemons (see p. 16),
chopped
1 teaspoon vanilla extract
1/4 cup (60 ml) Mint Syrup (see p. 8)

Preheat oven to 350°F (177°C). Grease and flour loaf
pan. Combine flour, baking powder, baking soda, and
salt in a small bowl. Set aside. Cream butter and sugar
until light and fluffy. Add eggs, one at a time, beating
briefly after each addition. Add yogurt, lemon, and
vanilla extract; mix. Fold in dry ingredients until just
incorporated. Pour batter into prepared pan. Bake 40 to
50 minutes until cake tester comes out clean. Let cake
cool 5 minutes. Unmold. Brush with Mint Syrup (p. 8).
Allow to cool completely.

NOTE: This cake is moist when first baked, but gets dry
quickly. Cake is best when eaten first or second day. For
future use freeze cake immediately after cooling.

MAKES 1 LOAF.

LIP-SMACKING COOKIES

"A kiss is just a kiss."

"La Belle Aurore" Pistachio Financiers

8 ounces (227 g) unsalted butter
2/3 cup (65 g) almond flour
2/3 cup (86 g) all-purpose flour
1 1/2 cup (180 g) confectioners' sugar
5 egg whites
1/2 teaspoon almond extract
2/3 cup (85 g) chopped pistachio nuts

Preheat oven to 450°F (232°C). Melt butter over medium heat in a small, heavy-bottomed saucepan. Continue cooking until butter turns a nut brown color, but do not let butter burn. Remove from heat. In a medium bowl, mix almond flour, flour, and sugar. Stir in egg whites with a whisk. Whisk in butter and almond extract until well blended. Stir in pistachio nuts. Grease and lightly flour 1 1/2-inch (38 mm) miniature muffin tins or small madeleine molds. Fill molds 2/3 full. Bake until golden brown, about 8 to 10 minutes. Unmold immediately.

MAKES 50 FINANCIERS.

Ferrari's Stuffed Apricots

RICK (to Ferrari): You're a fat hypocrite.

1/2 cup (100 g) almond paste
grated peel of 1 lemon
2 tablespoons lemon juice
3 tablespoons (15 g) dried, unsweetened coconut
1/4 cup (40 g) pistachio nuts, coarsely chopped
1/4 cup (40 g) unblanched, whole almonds, chopped
3 dozen dried, whole apricots

In a small bowl, mix almond paste with grated lemon peel and lemon juice. Add coconut. Coarsely chop pistachio nuts and almonds. Add to almond-paste mixture. Mix well. With a sharp paring knife, make a small slit in the side of each apricot. With index finger, open each apricot without making the slit any larger. Stuff each apricot with one level teaspoon of almond mixture. Refrigerate, covered until ready to serve. Please note that apricots will not completely close once stuffed.

MAKES 3 DOZEN.

Ilsa's Honey Almond Horns

12 ounces (340 g) unsalted butter
1 cup (120 g) confectioners' sugar
1/2 cup (150 g) honey
1 tablespoon vanilla extract
1/2 teaspoon salt
1 cup (120 g) ground almonds
3 cups (390 g) flour

Preheat oven to 325°F (162°C). Cream butter, sugar, honey, vanilla, and salt until light and fluffy. Fold in ground almonds and flour. Chill dough 30 minutes. Roll dough into tapered horns 3 inches (76 mm) by 1/2 inch (13 mm). Bake on ungreased cookie sheet at 325°F (162°C) for 10 minutes. Cookies are done when bottoms are a light golden color.

MAKES 5 DOZEN.

Captain Renault's Candied Citrus Rinds

RENAULT: Round up the usual suspects.

1 orange
1 grapefruit
1 1/2 cups (300 g) granulated sugar
4 ounces (114 g) bittersweet chocolate

Bring 2 quarts (2 liters) water to boil in a small non-aluminum saucepan. Carefully peel orange and grapefruits, keeping the pieces of peel as large as possible and leaving the white pith on the fruit. Cut the peel into 3 inch (76 mm) by 1/2 inch (13 mm) tapered strips. Immerse strips in saucepan filled with boiling water. When water returns to a boil, drain strips in colander and rinse with cold water. Place strips back into the saucepan—which is now empty—and add 1 1/4 cups (250 g) sugar and 1 1/4 cups water (300 ml). Bring to boil over medium heat. Allow to boil gently 45 minutes to 1 hour, or until grapefruit peel is translucent. Let cool in pot. Remove peel from syrup and place on cake rack to dry, 4 hours or more. Roll strips in remaining 1/4 cup (50 g) sugar. Melt chocolate in a bowl over hot water. Dip each strip in chocolate halfway. Let chocolate harden.

MAKES 50 PIECES.

Café Pierre's Almond Coconut Macaroons

1 1/2 cups (180 g) ground almonds
1 1/2 cups (100 g) dried, unsweetened coconut
2/3 cup (132 g) granulated sugar

4 egg whites
4 tablespoons coconut milk
1 teaspoon vanilla extract
1/2 teaspoon almond extract
20 dried apricot halves
20 dried date halves

Preheat oven to 350°F (177°C). In a medium bowl combine almonds, coconut, and sugar. In another bowl stir together egg whites, coconut milk, and extracts. Add egg white mixture to almond mixture, gradually stirring to make a sticky dough. Pinch off level-tablespoon-sized pieces of dough with wet hands. Form into boat-shaped mounds about 2 inches (50 mm) long. Place on cookie sheet lined with parchment or wax paper. Press an apricot or date half into the top of each macaroon. Bake for about 15 minutes, or until cookies are set but not brown. Remove from cookie sheet with a wet spatula.

MAKES ABOUT 3 DOZEN.

★ *Oscar Interlude* ★

What movies did Casablanca *beat for Best Picture of 1943?* For Whom the Bell Tolls, Heaven Can Wait, The Human Comedy, In Which We Serve, Madame Curie, The More the Merrier, The Ox-Bow Incident, The Song of Bernadette, and Watch on the Rhine.

Humphrey Bogart was nominated for Best Actor in Casablanca *(he lost to Paul Lukas in* Watch on the Rhine*); that same year Ingrid Bergman was also nominated for Best Actress, but for what movie?* For Whom the Bell Tolls *(she lost to Jennifer Jones in* The Song of Bernadette*).*

The Leuchtags' Streusel Fig Bars

MR. LEUCHTAG: Liebchen, uh, sweetness heart, what watch?
MRS. LEUCHTAG (glancing at her wristwatch): Ten watch.
MR. LEUCHTAG (surprised): Such much?
CARL: Er, you will get along beautifully in America, huh.

4 ounces (114 g) unsalted butter at room temperature
3 tablespoons granulated sugar
grated rind of 1 lemon
1 egg
1 1/2 cups (195 g) all-purpose flour
1/4 teaspoon baking powder
1/4 teaspoon baking soda
1/4 cup (40 g) raspberry jam
1 recipe Fig Compote
1 recipe Honey Streusel Topping

Preheat oven to 350°F (177°C). Cream butter and sugar together until light and fluffy. Add rind and egg, beating well. Fold in flour, baking powder, and baking soda. Chill dough for 15 minutes. Roll out to a rectangle 9 by 13 inches (23 x 33 cm) and 1/4 inch (6 mm) thick onto wax paper. Place paper with rolled dough onto a cookie sheet. Spread dough with raspberry jam and Fig Compote. Sprinkle with Honey Streusel Topping. Bake at 350°F (177°C) for 20 to 25 minutes or until oats begin to brown. Let cool. Cut into 4 by 1-inch (10 x 3 cm) bars.

MAKES 20 BARS.

FIG COMPOTE
3/4 pound (340 g) dried black mission figs, diced
6 tablespoons (112 g) honey
2 tablespoons lemon juice

2 tablespoons orange juice
1/2 cup (120 ml) water

Put all ingredients into a medium non-aluminum saucepan. Bring slowly to boil over medium heat. Let boil until liquid is reduced and starts to glaze figs, about 15 minutes.

HONEY STREUSEL TOPPING
3 ounces (85 g) unsalted butter
3 tablespoons brown sugar
3 tablespoons honey
1 1/2 teaspoons lemon juice
1 1/2 (120 g) cups oats

Melt butter in a medium saucepan over low heat. Add brown sugar, honey, and lemon juice. Bring slowly to a boil. Add oats and stir. Remove from heat and let cool.

Sam's Chocolate Truffle Kisses

12 ounces (340 g) chopped semi-sweet chocolate or
chocolate chips
1 cup (240 ml) heavy cream
1 teaspoon ground cinnamon

Place chocolate in a medium bowl. Bring cream to boil and pour over the chocolate. Whisk until mixture is smooth. Whisk in cinnamon. Refrigerate for 45 minutes, stirring every 5 minutes. After 45 minutes chocolate should be thick enough to form stiff peaks. (If not, continue to chill until it reaches that point.) Spoon mixture into pastry bag and pipe chocolate into petit-four paper liners, in 1 1/2-inch (38 mm) kisses. Refrigerate until firm, at least one hour.

MAKES ABOUT 60 KISSES.

Ricky's Sesame Anise Cookies

RICK: Louis, whatever gave you the impression that I might be interested in helping Laszlo escape?
RENAULT: Because, my dear Ricky, I suspect that under that cynical shell you're at heart a semtimentalist.

4 ounces (114 g) unsalted butter
2 tablespoons toasted sesame seeds
1 teaspoon crushed anise seeds
1 egg
2/3 cup (80 g) confectioners' sugar
1/2 teaspoon anise extract
1 1/3 cups (170 g) flour
1/2 teaspoon baking powder
1 pinch salt

MIX TO ROLL COOKIES IN:
1/4 cup (30 g) confectioners' sugar
1/4 cup (35 g) toasted sesame seeds

Preheat oven to 350°F (177°C). Melt butter in small saucepan with sesame and anise seeds. Beat egg and confectioners' sugar until light and fluffy. Add butter mixture and continue to beat 1 minute. Add anise extract. Sift flour, baking powder, and salt over egg mixture. Fold in by hand to form a smooth dough. Pinch off tablespoon-sized pieces of dough and roll into 3-inch (76 mm) long logs with tapered ends. Roll each log in sugar/sesame seed mixture. Place logs on cookie sheet lined with wax paper. Bake 15 to 17 minutes, until cookies begin to crack slightly on top. Do not allow cookies to color.

These are good cookies to serve w   The texture is
similar to biscotti cookies.

MAKES 3 1/2 DOZEN COOKIES.

New World Orange Butter Cookies

8 ounces (227 g) unsalted butter
2/3 cup (132 g) granulated sugar
grated rind of 2 medium oranges
1/2 cup (60 g) ground almonds
1 teaspoon orange flower water
2 egg yolks
2 tablespoons orange juice
1 1/2 cups (195 g) flour

Preheat oven to 325°F (164°C). Cream butter, sugar and
orange peel until light and fluffy. Add ground almonds,
flower water, egg yolk, and orange juice. Beat until well
blended. Fold in flour until just incorporated. Drop batter by well-rounded teaspoonfuls onto a cookie sheet
lined with parchment or wax paper. Bake 14 to 15 minutes until edges begin to brown.

MAKES 3 DOZEN COOKIES.

Orange Coriander Cookies

To above batter, add 8 teaspoons crushed coriander
seeds. (Crush seeds by using a rolling pin or the bottom
of heavy pan.) These crunchy cookies have a unusual,
fragrant flavor.

"As Time Goes By" Preserved Lemon Cookies

6 ounces (170 g) unsalted butter
$^2/_3$ cup (80 g) confectioners' sugar
$^3/_4$ cup (75 g) almond flour
1 egg
3 tablespoons Sugar-Preserved Lemons (see p. 16),
finely chopped
1 tablespoon lemon juice
1 $^1/_2$ cups (195 g) flour

Preheat oven to 325°F (162°C). Cream butter and sugar until light and fluffy. Add almond flour and mix well. Add egg, preserved lemon, and lemon juice. Fold in flour. Roll dough into 2 8-inch (20 cm) logs. Refrigerate until firm, about 30 minutes. Slice cookies 1/4 inch (6 mm) thick. Bake for 10 to 12 minutes on cookie sheets lined with parchment or wax paper. Cookies are done when set but not browned.

MAKES ABOUT 50 COOKIES.

★ Trivia Finale ★

When the Marx Brothers were filming A Night in Casablanca *in 1946, they received a threatening letter from the Warner Bros. legal department, to which Groucho replied: "I had no idea that the city of Casablanca belonged exclusively to Warner Bros....You probably have the right to use the name Warners, but what about Brothers? Professionally, we were brothers long before you were."*